# Old KIRKCALDY
## Central, North & West
*by*
### Eric Eunson

WILKIE'S Boots & Shoes are correct for Quality, Comfort & Wear. Address, 90 Mid Street, Pathhead. and 66 Dunnikier Road, Kirkcaldy.

William Wilkie founded his boot and shoe business in premises at 90 Mid Street, Pathhead around 1894. By 1900 it was in the hands of his son John, who had opened a second shop at 66 Dunnikier Road before 1906. The Pathhead branch closed before 1920, although the Dunnikier Road premises remained in business until around 1930.

© Eric Eunson 1998
First published in the United Kingdom, 1998,
reprinted 2005, 2010
by Stenlake Publishing Ltd.
01290 551122
www.stenlake.co.uk

ISBN 9781840330526

# ACKNOWLEDGEMENTS

I would like to thank the staff of the reference department of Kirkcaldy Central Library for their valuable assistance in researching this book; also Bill Fiet of Leslie for help with additional information and permission to use the following pictures: inside front cover, title page, and pages 7, 9, 44 and 45.

THE PUBLISHERS REGRET THAT THEY CANNOT SUPPLY
COPIES OF ANY PICTURES FEATURED IN THIS BOOK.

# BIBLIOGRAPHY

Bennett, G. P., *The Great Road Between Forth and Tay*
Brotchie, Alan, *Fife's Trams and Buses*, 1990
Fife Regional Council, *Kirkcaldy Street Origins*, 1975
Gifford, John, *The Buildings of Scotland, Fife*, 1988
MacBean, L., *Kirkcaldy Burgh Records*, 1908
Mackay, A. J. G., *Fife and Kinross*, 1896
Scott Bruce, William, *The Railways of Fife*, 1980
Torrie, E. P. D. & Coleman, R., *Historic Kirkcaldy*, 1995
Wilkie, James, *History of Fife*, 1923
*Statistical Accounts*, Parishes of Abbotshall (1791 and 1836) and Kirkcaldy (1795, 1843 and 1951)

# INTRODUCTION

This book includes the old royal burgh of Kirkcaldy, Linktown to the west, and the suburbs which developed to the north of the town from the nineteenth century onwards. Although the discovery of human remains and artefacts dating back to the Bronze Age suggest some four millennia of occupation, Kirkcaldy does not appear in recorded history until 1075, during the reign of Malcolm III (1058-1093) who granted the town and shire of Kirkcaldy to the newly founded Abbey of Dunfermline. The parish church was founded during the reign of David I (1124-1153) and was reconsecrated in 1244 by David de Bernham, Bishop of St Andrews. Scotland was occupied by the English from 1296 to 1306 and in 1304 the Abbot of Dunfermline sought permission from Edward I to establish an annual fair and weekly market in Kirkcaldy; these privileges were granted the following year. Kirkcaldy was raised in status from a township to a burgh in the reign of Robert I (1306-1329). In 1451 the Abbot granted it feu ferme rights, which meant that the town gained control of all its revenues upon an annual payment to the abbey of 33s 4d.

By the beginning of the sixteenth century the town had become an important trading port, and records note that wood was landed at the harbour bound for both Edinburgh Castle and Falkland Palace, as well as for shipbuilding. In 1559 Kirkcaldy was sacked and burned by French soldiers in the service of Mary of Lorraine, who were ravaging the wealthy burghs of the Fife coast on account of their leanings towards Protestantism. The town is noted as having 28 salt pans in 1573. Salt was a valuable commodity, essential for preserving meat, and could only be extracted by boiling sea water. This was done by heating it in large rectangular pans made from iron plates. The fuel needed in this process was small coal, from which it is safe to deduce that coal was also being worked in the immediate vicinity of the burgh by this time.

The population of the town was composed of two classes, the burgesses, licensed to practice their particular trades, own property and vote for the election of the burgh officials known as baillies; and everybody else, who basically had no rights whatsoever. The privileges of the burgesses were jealously guarded, and each trade strictly regulated its own numbers. Laws were passed which forbade the residents of Kirkcaldy from buying goods from merchants or artisans in the neighbouring villages of Pathhead and Linktown and a further law of 1594 dictated that any Kirkcaldy burgess who went to live in either of these places would lose all his rights. This system of commercial protectionism remained in place until 1722.

In 1584 a visiting ship brought a plague, believed to be cholera or typhus, to Fife, which claimed 300 lives in Kirkcaldy. Although not as zealous in its persecution of witches as Dysart, several women stood accused in 1597 and in 1604 Dorothy Oliphant was found guilty of the crime and banished from the burgh. Only two people are actually known to have been executed for witchcraft, Alison Dick and her husband William Coke, who were burned at the stake in 1633.

In 1616 the population of Kirkcaldy was 3,147, and in 1644 100 ships belonged to the port. It received a confirmation of royal burgh status from Charles I in the same year, but when this title was first conferred is unknown, the original charter being lost. In 1650 the parish of Kirkcaldy was split in two. The largest portion became the new parish of Abbotshall, containing Linktown; Kirkcaldy parish itself was reduced to a small area of ground around the town, which then comprised a single street stretching from the Port Brae to Milton Road.

The seventeenth century history of Kirkcaldy is a catalogue of disasters. The town supported the Covenanting cause and in 1645 lost 200 men at the battle of Kilsyth. This was closely followed by the Civil War which brought Kirkcaldy to the brink of ruin. By 1650 nearly 500 burgesses were reported killed and 58 ships had been seized or sunk. Only a dozen ships were registered to the port by 1656 and of these only six were owned by Kirkcaldy men. Despite this, from 1665 to 1668 the burgh was rated sixth in the taxation roll of Scotland and was expected to contribute one fortieth of the total national revenue. Nonetheless, by 1668 the town's debts amounted to over £3,000. In 1662 the council voted that no one should be admitted as a new burgess unless they first spent 500 merks on building a ship, and by 1673 the town had a fleet of 25 vessels. In 1692, however, it was stated that 19 ships had been lost in the preceding decade.

The eighteenth century opened as traumatically as its predecessor, when the town was looted and burned by Highland Jacobites under McIntosh in 1715. Luckily, this event was followed by prolonged peace and a period of growth and consolidation for Kirkcaldy. The handloom weaving industry, introduced to the town in 1672, flourished, and between 1733 and 1743 output of finished linen rose from 177,000 to 316,000 yards. In 1739 the town introduced a large annual linen market which included city merchants among its customers. Leather making commenced in 1723. Shipping, however, was slow to recover and in 1760 the town possessed only three boats – two ferries and a vessel engaged in the coasting trade. In 1778 Kirkcaldy revived its shipbuilding industry and seventeen years later boasted 26 square riggers, one sloop and two ferries. The town's first mill for spinning cotton opened in 1784 and within eight years employed 110 hands.

In the late eighteenth century the salt industry declined on both sides of the Firth and was discontinued in Kirkcaldy for a brief period before 1795, owing to the exhaustion of the mines which supplied the pans with coal. The saltworks restarted in 1795 when a sharp rise in the price of salt made it economical to import coal from other areas. Many saltworks on the Forth ceased operating in the early nineteenth century, but salt continued to be made at Kirkcaldy until the mid-1930s, although the industry adapted from producing sea salt to refining rock salt brought from mines in Cheshire.

Fife's roads were generally in very poor condition until the late eighteenth century, hindering commerce and communication. The Government sought to improve matters by passing a series of Acts for the setting up of turnpike boards; groups of landowners and entrepreneurs who would privately finance the building of new, quality roads. The construction and maintenance of these was paid for by means of tolls levied at intervals along the route. A turnpike road from the Pettycur ferry to Cupar and the north was authorised in 1790 and another from Gallatown to Crail was begun in the same year. Both brought a huge increase in the volume of traffic passing along Kirkcaldy High Street and encouraged the development of the town. Kirkcaldy also lay on the route of the first public coach service in Fife, which commenced in 1805. Forty years later it had daily coaches either passing through or commencing in the town, providing direct links with Aberdeen, Dundee, Perth, Glasgow and St Andrews.

A paddle steamer was introduced on the ferry passage between Pettycur and Newhaven in 1820, and similar vessels were placed on the crossings from Kirkcaldy and Burntisland the following year. Kirkcaldy became an important ferry port and by 1845 offered eight steamer crossings per day in summer and six in winter. The arrival of the railway in 1847 brought about the decline of the Kirkcaldy ferry, which gradually became an excursion service before stopping altogether in 1857.

By 1845 91 ships belonged to the town, among them several engaged in whaling in the Arctic Ocean. The first Kirkcaldy ship to take up whaling was the *Earl Percy* in 1813; the last was the *Brilliant*, sold to Peterhead in 1866. A whale oil factory was set up on the foreshore below Ravenscraig Castle and following the collapse of the industry was converted into the Ravenscraig Chemical Works. The factory was abandoned early this century.

In 1828 a young man named Michael Nairn set himself up as a canvas manufacturer in Kirkcaldy, turning his attention to making floorcloth in 1847. He established a factory in Nether Street, Pathhead in the same year. In 1860 a Yorkshireman, Fred Walton, invented a new floor covering which he patented as linoleum, from the Latin names (*linum* and *oleum*) of its principal constituents, flax and oil. Nairn took out a licence to manufacture Walton's patent and expanded his Pathhead works. Many were sceptical about the venture and the factory became known as 'Nairn's Folly'. But the rest, as they say, is history, and for the next 100 years Kirkcaldy remained the world's largest producer of linoleum. In 1951 Nairn's had ten factories in Kirkcaldy, seven making lino, one making floorcloth, a paper mill and a canvas works. A second large linoleum factory, the Caledonia Works, was established to the north of the railway by Messrs Shepherd, Beveridge and Barry in 1874. This also prospered and had developed a huge complex of buildings around the original factory by 1900.

The effect of ribbon development along the turnpikes, and the population growth caused by industrial expansion, meant that by 1850 Kirkcaldy had merged into one contiguous mass with neighbouring Linktown, Pathhead, Sinclairtown and Gallatown. In 1876 the burgh of Kirkcaldy formally annexed these adjoining places along with a large chunk of the parish of Abbotshall, allowing the town to develop beyond its cramped seventeenth century boundaries.

Many of Kirkcaldy's public buildings were built or rebuilt in the late nineteenth century, most of them by the town's linoleum magnates. When Michael Beveridge died in 1890 he left a bequest of £50,000 to be used for the laying out of a public park and the building of a public hall. Long known as the Adam Smith and Beveridge Hall, it is now just called the Adam Smith Centre, an unfortunate snub to Mr Beveridge's generosity. The second Michael Nairn gave his home town a hospital in 1890 and a new high school in 1894. His son funded the building of the war memorial and museum in 1925 and added the library in 1928. He bought Dysart House in 1929 and immediately gave the grounds, now Ravenscraig Park, to the town.

In 1930 brave little Dysart, which had long held out against annexation, was brought into the burgh of Kirkcaldy and in 1931 the population of the combined burghs was 46,019. The burgh boundary was extended to take in Boreland in 1939. After the war Kirkcaldy, like most other towns in Britain, had a housing shortage and it was decided to extend the burgh boundary out to Chapel in 1949 to provide more land for development. Between 1951 and 1965 Wimpey built 2,000 local authority houses within the burgh. They were also the largest single developer of private homes and work on their Dunnikier Estate began in 1961.

Radical redevelopment of the town and its suburbs was first proposed in 1951. What followed was the systematic destruction of all Kirkcaldy's antique quarters, with four centuries of burgh architecture swept away in as many decades. Sadly, conservation has always been a very low priority to the town's administrators. A recent National Lottery grant has secured the future of a threatened sixteenth century merchant's house at 339-343 High Street, but it is sad to note that buildings of a similar age were torn down in a road widening scheme at the Port Brae less than a decade ago. In 1998 one of the last remaining seventeenth century buildings in the High Street, at the foot of Kirk Wynd, was pulled down, although a replica is proposed in its place. There are several fine buildings in the town which are at risk, and those concerned with preserving what history it retains cannot afford to be complacent.

Kirkcaldy's population reached a peak of 53,750 in 1961. During the 1960s the world demand for linoleum declined steadily as plastic floor coverings were developed. The works of Barry, Ostlere and Shepherd closed in 1964, and Nairn's Pathhead factories soon joined them. Over the next thirty years most of the town's staple industries either downsized or closed altogether, the effects of which are indicated by a fall in population to 47,962 by 1981. The same decade witnessed the closure of the town's industrial museum during a wave of council cutbacks.

Today Kirkcaldy is the principal service and entertainment centre in the county and continues to be a focus for new housing and retail development. It faces problems common to all Scotland's former industrial towns, and how it will meet the challenges these present remains to be seen.

References to Kirkcaldy Harbour can be traced back at least as far as the mid-fifteenth century, although there is no reason to doubt the belief of many writers that the natural anchorage at the mouth of the East Burn has been used as a shelter for boats since the town began to develop in the Dark Ages. The East Pier is the oldest (although any early stonework has been obscured by Victorian masonry), and was built on an area once known as the Monkcraig. The pier was taken down and rebuilt between 1587 and 1600; breaches were repaired in 1663, but it was badly damaged by storms in 1717 and remained ruinous for some years thereafter. In 1752 a West Pier was added; this was extended four years later. The baillies passed a regulation forbidding ships from dumping their ballast in the haven in 1595. This picture dates from 1905.

Improvements to the harbour were carried out between 1843 and 1846 to plans prepared by the Largo-born civil engineer, James Leslie. The East Pier was lengthened and its tip made broader to accommodate a railway terminus, in anticipation of the arrival of the Edinburgh and Northern Railway in 1847. Leslie also designed the spur from the main line to the harbour, some supporting arches of which can still be seen at the bottom of the Path. The harbour was enlarged again between 1906 and 1908 by Rendell and Robertson, who further extended the East Pier and reconstructed the harbour as a dock and outer harbour. This aerial photograph was taken in the early 1920s.

*At the Harbour — Kirkcaldy*

The tall building on the right of this late 1920s view was the St Mary's Canvas Works, which belonged to Nairn's Linoleum. The main block was built in 1914 west of a neighbouring single-storey works of 1864. The facade of the older block was retained after it closed, and along with the adjoining frontage of the Union Chapel is to be used as a curtain wall for a new annexe of Fife College which currently under construction. The harbour swing bridge in the foreground was built by the Brandon Bridge Building Company and dates from the 1906 improvements.

99485 J.V.

The Harbour, Kirkcaldy

Most of Kirkcaldy's nineteenth century industries chose sites close to the railway, and the bulk of the goods traffic through the harbour was connected with Nairn's linoleum works in Pathhead. Incoming ships brought cargoes of cork and other raw materials, and finished bales of lino were exported to every corner of the globe. As the linoleum industry declined, ships became a rare site in the harbour. This photograph of the inner basin dates from 1926. At the time of writing it looks as if controversial plans to fill in the whole harbour and redevelop the site with housing and shops are set to receive planning approval.

This Southampton seaplane was an unusual visitor to Kirkcaldy Harbour in the late 1920s. It was attached to 201 Squadron RAF based at Calshot in Hampshire and was taking part in a long distance test flight, which also included calls at Oban and Scapa in Orkney. This type of aircraft was used by the RAF from 1925 to 1936 and had a wing span of 75 feet. 201 Squadron are still operational today and are now based at RAF Kinloss.

The Battery, Kirkcaldy.

The corner of Charlotte Street on the left serves to locate this almost unrecognisable 1903 view, looking east along the Esplanade. The cannons belonged to the Kirkcaldy section of the 1st Fifeshire Royal Garrison Artillery. Yeomanry battalions such as this one were formed when the Government decided that towns should raise volunteer forces in the wake of the Crimean War (1853-1856). The cannons were usually kept in the garrison's hall in Hunter Street, and were only brought out for firing practice. They became redundant in 1901 when the War Office dictated that all volunteers should be trained on the modern big guns they had installed at Kinghorn and Pettycur. Colonel Johnston donated two of the cannons to the council, who placed them in Beveridge Park where they remained until 1941 when they were taken away for scrap. The 1st Fifeshire RGA was absorbed into the Territorial Army along with all Britain's volunteer battalions in 1908.

The sea wall and Esplanade were built during 1921-1922 to relieve post-war unemployment. The Esplanade soon developed as the town's main bus stance, but no shelter was provided for waiting passengers until 1951 when Alexanders built the bus station shown in this photograph. In 1958 a second bus station was built beside the Town House. This served the town's internal network, and the Esplanade became the terminus for out of town services. Country passengers still had to use the ill-appointed Esplanade station until 1981 when the other station was enlarged to accommodate all services. Although this was refurbished in 1993, its architect was clearly more concerned with the thwarting of vandals than the comfort of passengers!

HIGH STREET, EAST

The tall building on the left hand side of this Edwardian view was the King's Playhouse theatre. Opened on 14 November 1904, it could seat 2,000 people with standing room for 500 more. Its roof was designed to slide back for ventilation, meaning that the audience could literally see the stars from the stalls. Initially it staged a mixture of musical comedies and drama, but these proved unpopular with the public. Built at a cost of £20,000, it was sold in 1908 for just £7,000 to a Glasgow entertainment magnate named Bostock. He renamed the theatre the Hippodrome and turned it into a music hall; it became the Opera House in 1916. In 1937 it was turned into the Regal Cinema, later becoming the ABC, in which guise it survives to this day.

Henry Morton Barnett was provost of Kirkcaldy from 1903 to 1907 and owner of one of the town's best-known shops, Barnett & Morton, ironmongers. The business was founded in 1821 by his father John, who specialised in the manufacture of weigh beams and mangles. The Morton portion of the name was supplied by his brother-in-law James Morton, who was a partner in the firm from 1856 until his death in 1864. In 1895 the business moved

HENRY M. BARNET,
PROVOST OF KIRKCALDY.

"FIFESHIRE ADVERTISER"
PICTURE CARDS.

No. 7.

into premises at 192-195 High Street where the established name remained over the door until House of Fraser took over the company, which it kept on as a going concern, in 1975. In 1988 this company was taken over by Arnotts, who promptly closed the Kirkcaldy store.

Old Dunnikier House stood at the south-west corner of Oswald's Wynd and the High Street. It was built by John Oswald in the late seventeenth century. In 1703 his son, Captain James Oswald, bought the estate of Dunnikier, hence the name of the family town house. Note the similarity between its tower and the contemporary bell tower of Dysart tollbooth. The western half of this venerable old house was torn down in 1907 to make way for a new shop for Kirkcaldy Co-operative Society. The rest of the house stood until 1966 when it was demolished to extend the Co-op, itself completely destroyed by fire in the early 1970s.

High Street, looking East, Kirkcaldy.

The High Street looked much the same in 1960 as it did when this picture postcard was published in 1907. Redevelopment of the town centre was first proposed in 1964 and within a decade most of the buildings on the left of the picture, spanning some 300 years, had been torn down. Their replacements are quite devoid of charm. The foot of Kirk Wynd, in the background, is believed to have been the site of the burgh's medieval market place and mercat cross. The cross was topped with a lion and unicorn, and was repaired in 1669. It was removed by the town council in 1737.

14

Tollbooth Street is on the right of this photograph showing the High Street decorated for the Coronation of King George VI and Queen Elizabeth on 12 May 1937. The location of the burgh's medieval tollbooth, which served as council chambers, armoury and prison, has not been identified, but may well have been in the vicinity of the market place at the foot of Kirk Wynd. A map of 1824 shows a building on the east side of Tollbooth Street, two buildings down from the High Street, described as the tollbooth. In 1826 the tollbooth was replaced by a custom-built town hall, a fragment of which can be seen on the extreme right of the picture.

FOOT OF WHYTE'S CAUSEWAY, KIRKCALDY.

Kirkcaldy Corporation Tramway ran its first car on 23 February 1903 from the Gallatown terminus, via St Clair Street, High Street and Linktown. The trams proved a hit with postcard publishers in the town, as illustrated by this example, published by M. & L. Page in 1905. Whyte's Causeway is named after Robert Whyte, elected first provost of the town in 1657. In 1588 the baillies and burgesses of Kirkcaldy had sworn the town would never be governed by a provost, as such an official would be 'a danger and an inconvenience' and bring 'servitude and slaverie' upon the town.

Art deco architecture is in evidence in this 1953 view of the High Street looking east from the foot of Whytehouse Avenue. The Burton building was built in 1935 and the long established premises of J. & A. Grieve, outfitters and milliners, were given a modern overhaul around the same date. A one-way traffic system, imposed on the High Street in 1965, proved only a limited solution to the congestion problem in the town centre. In the mid-1980s the area from Whytehouse Avenue to Kirk Wynd was declared a pedestrian precinct, with a mixed response from local traders. However, despite misgivings the traffic-free environment ultimately proved popular with shoppers, and it is conspicuous that the areas at both ends of the street which are full of empty shops are those which lie outwith the pedestrianised zone.

Graham & Co.'s china shop at the bottom of Whytehouse Avenue, photographed in 1928. Built around 1905, it is the only single-storey building on the High Street, an unusually uneconomical use of such a valuable building plot. This was a favourite trysting place where young hopefuls would wait to meet their dates – or be stood up! The business is still trading today under the name Lawley's.

High Street, looking West, Kirkcaldy.

Whytehouse Mansions, on the right of this 1907 view, were built between 1895 and 1898 and designed by John Little. They were the largest single development of buildings on the High Street until the erection of modern shopping malls in the 1980s. The row stands on what was once the street frontage of the gardens of Whyte House, a small Georgian mansion with a pillared portico approached by a sweeping staircase. Built around 1790, the house remained standing in the yard of Carlton Bakery until permission was granted for its demolition in 1997.

01838 JV

The spire on the left of this 1905 picture belongs to the West End Congregational Church, built in 1874. On the right is the Abbotshall Free Church, dating from 1869 and deprived of its spire in the 1970s when it was converted into a shop. The two-storey eighteenth century buildings closest to this church were replaced by a three-storey tenement with shops on the ground floor before 1907. Those closest to the camera were replaced by a Safeway supermarket; the shop is now closed and the building looks shabbier with each month that passes.

Wemyss Buildings, incorporating the Olympia Arcade, and the adjoining eighteenth century building are the only landmarks remaining from this 1905 scene. Built around 1900, the arcade is home to several small speciality businesses and provides a welcome break from the chain store dominated High Street. The town's West Port stood in this area. It was one of three gateways to the medieval burgh, the others being in the vicinity of the Port Brae and the head of Kirk Wynd. In 1669 the baillies ordered that Kirkcaldy's fleshmarket be moved from its site beside the Balcanquhal Burn in the town centre (now George Burn Wynd), to the West Port.

James Tough, a well-known Kirkcaldy nurseryman and seed merchant, photographed by Robert Douglas in 1866. Tough was born in Banff *c*.1792 and established himself as a seedsman in Kirkcaldy in 1823, setting up shop at 155 High Street. Some time after 1843 he moved his business to 177 High Street and remained there until 1865 when he sold the concern to his competitor Edward Sang. Sang's was one of the town's most enduring businesses, lasting from 1791 to 1974.

Kirkcaldy worthy Jimmy 'Boxer' Lyndsay and his donkey Persimmon, photographed in 1905. Lyndsay was a cadger who sold fish throughout the town from a donkey cart until his death *c*.1914. Man and beast lived together in a stable belonging to Dr Curror's house, Viewforth Tower, a long-vanished Linktown landmark. Lyndsay was partial to a beer while he worked, which he would share with his four legged friend. When his old donkey died, worn out from a lifetime of pulling a cart that was too large for it, he was given another which he named Persimmon, after King Edward VII's horse which had just won the Derby.

The west end of the Esplanade is the setting for this 1905 picture of the Links Market. The market can trace its origins back to 1305, when Edward I granted the Abbey of Dunfermline the right to hold a weekly market and annual fair in Kirkcaldy. When Charles I made the town a royal burgh in 1644, its charter contained the right to hold two annual fairs, although these had ceased long before 1795. The Links Market is the successor of one of two annual fairs formerly held in Linktown, a privilege granted by Charles II in 1672. The market was held in Links Street until the opening of the tramway in 1903, when it was moved to the Sands Road (now the Esplanade).

Traditional helter-skelters photographed at the Links Market on 23 April 1956. The 'Mountain Glide' belonged to Joe Leonard, the other ride to S. Maynes. The price of a few seconds sliding downhill on a mat was sixpence, a reminder that even forty years ago a trip to the market was a costly affair. Throughout this century the Links Market has grown steadily in size and it is now celebrated as Europe's longest street fair. Its arrival each April is also known locally as the harbinger of a week of wet and windy weather!

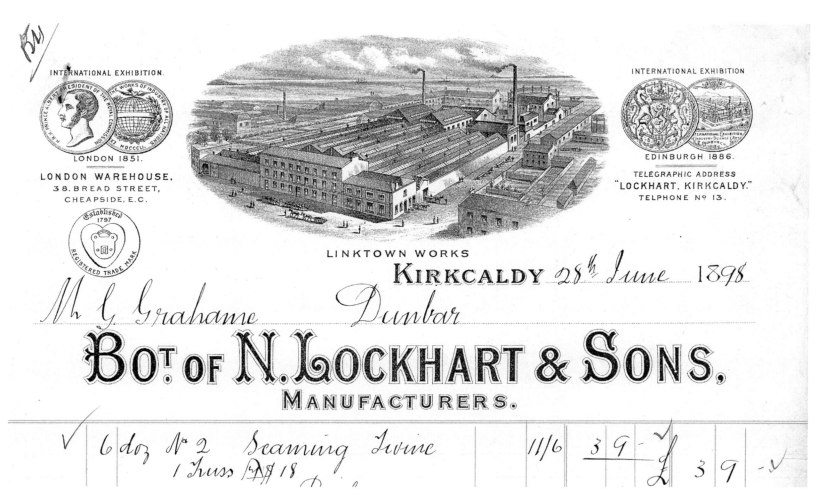

INTERNATIONAL EXHIBITION.

H.R.H. PRINCE ALBERT PRESIDENT OF THE ROYAL COMMISSION. EX. MDCCCLI. THE WORKS OF INDUSTRY OF ALL NATIONS.

LONDON 1851.

LONDON WAREHOUSE,
38, BREAD STREET,
CHEAPSIDE, E.C.

Established 1797
REGISTERED TRADE MARK

LINKTOWN WORKS

INTERNATIONAL EXHIBITION

EDINBURGH 1886.

INTERNATIONAL EXHIBITION INDUSTRY SCIENCE & ART EDINBVRGH 1886.

TELEGRAPHIC ADDRESS
"LOCKHART, KIRKCALDY."
TELPHONE Nº 13.

KIRKCALDY 28ᵗʰ June 1898

Mʳ G Grahame          Dunbar

# Bot. OF N. LOCKHART & SONS,
## MANUFACTURERS.

| | | | | | | | | | |
|---|---|---|---|---|---|---|---|---|---|
| ✓ | 6 | doz | Nº 2 Seaming Twine | | 11/6 | 3 | 9 | - | ✓ |
| | | | 1 Truss | | | | | | |
| | | | | | | 3 | 9 | - | ✓ |

Founded in 1789, Ninian Lockhart's Linktown works was the first linen factory to open in Fife. His sons James and Robert installed the factory's first power looms in 1857. One of the products made by the firm was 'Lockhart's Stripes', a fabric favoured by fishwives. In more recent years souvenir tea towels were a speciality. In 1979 Lockhart's took over Richmond Brothers, a competing Dundee firm, but the Linktown works closed two years later. The company continued to operate from a former flax mill in Abbotshall Road it had acquired some years earlier, but shut down completely in 1982. All the buildings on the Linktown site were cleared in 1985.

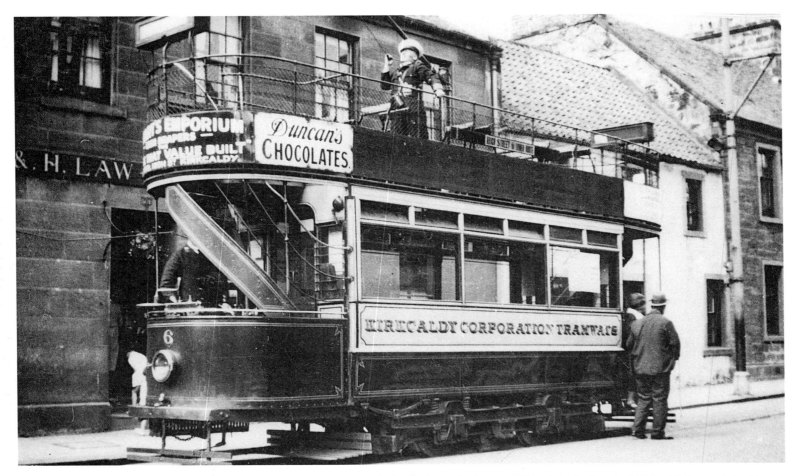

Car number six, photographed outside A. & H. Law's grocery shop at 100 Links Street in the late 1920s. The first part of Kirkcaldy's municipal tramway opened on 23 February 1903, and eight months later a second route opened from Junction Road to Whytescauseway and Beveridge Park Gates. In many parts of the town narrow streets meant that only a single track could be laid, and this created the need for numerous passing loops. These caused delays and by the 1920s the ill-maintained tramway had become a byword for inefficiency. Competition from bus services began after the Great War and increased throughout the twenties. In 1931 the town council sold the tramway to Alexanders of Falkirk, who were in the process of acquiring a monopoly of Fife's bus companies. Kirkcaldy's last tram ran on 15 May 1931.

Every district of Kirkcaldy supported several amateur football teams when this 1907 picture was taken in the Linktown. Unfortunately the only one of the group who has been identified is Robert Hutchison, standing with the towel at the extreme left of the back row.

AVA STREET, KIRKCALDY.

Ava Street was built around 1900 on the site of Newton Park, which had contained a football field and cycling track. The street was named in honour of Lady Helen Hermione, the wife of Robert Munro Ferguson of Raith and daughter of the First Marquis of Dufferin and Ava.

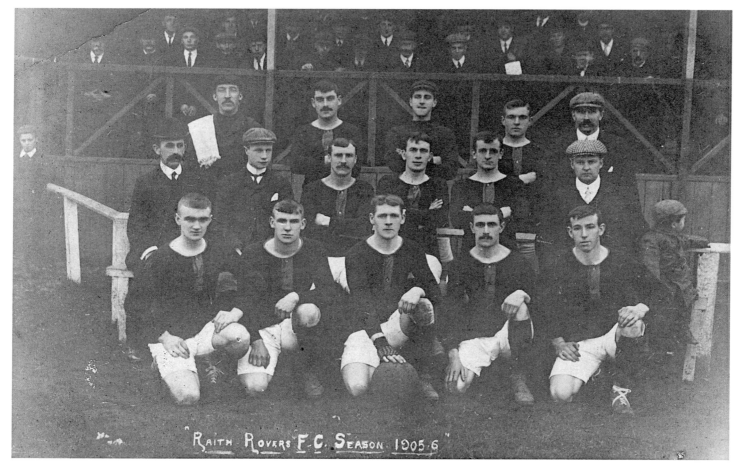

Raith Rovers were founded in 1883 and initially played on the Sands Brae, now part of the Esplanade. Later on they used an old claypit near their present ground, but were forced to vacate this in 1891 when it was incorporated into Beveridge Park. In the same year they moved to Stark's Park, named after its owner, Councillor Robert Stark, a rope manufacturer and licensee at West Bridge. The ground was previously used by several other teams, and in 1887 Stark used a novel technique to clear the pitch of an invasion by rival fans, releasing a bull he kept in a byre nearby! The first grandstand was built in 1896 and in 1902 Raith became the first Fife club to join the league. The club entered the First Division in 1910, achieving third position in 1923. Raith were relegated six years later, but achieved promotion once again in 1948.

The first congregation of Inverteil Parish Church was formed in 1856. They worshipped in a barn in Mill Street before moving into their own church, built to a design by Campbell Douglas, in 1857. In 1991 the building was sold to the Coptic Orthodox Church and is the first church belonging to this faith in Scotland. The world's oldest Christian sect, the Coptic Orthodox Church traces its origins back to the martyrdom of St Mark in Egypt in the first century AD. The former Inverteil Church was reconsecrated by Pope Shenoudah III in 1992.

Abbotshall Parish Church was built in 1788 and a date stone of 1674 from its predecessor is included in the spire. The interior was completely redesigned in 1970 and the fabric restored in 1984. The inset portrait in this Edwardian postcard is of the Reverend Bruce Beveridge Begg (1837-1923), minister of Abbotshall from 1865 to 1911.

Kirkcaldy's police constable number 43, photographed by G. Thomson of 82 High Street in the 1880s. The police station and cells were originally situated in the Town House, which was built in 1826 and stood on the site of Marks and Spencer's shop. The police moved into their present station in St Brycedale Avenue in 1902.

The sheriff court was designed by James Gillespie in Scottish baronial style and was completed in 1884. The builder was George Smith, an important Kirkcaldy contractor, who was also responsible for McIntosh's furniture factory and many of the town's linoleum works. An extension added to the court in 1982 does nothing to complement the original building.

POST OFFICE. KIRKCALDY.

In 1603 James VI established a series of posting stations from Berwick to Edinburgh, where fresh horses were to be maintained for the transmission of royal correspondence. By 1627 this relay had been extended across the Forth, and Kirkcaldy burgh minutes record the proposed auction of the position of postmaster in that year. This was an exclusively royal service, and a public post office did not open in the town until 1715, when the first postmaster was Robert Roxburgh. The post office was housed in a variety of premises on the High Street before it moved to this building on the corner of Hunter Street in 1902, photographed about five years later. In 1994 counter facilities were transferred to the William Low supermarket in the Postings and the former post office was put up for sale. It opened as the Old Post Hotel in 1996.

Two railways passing through Kirkcaldy were proposed in 1836, but neither scheme attracted sufficient capital to proceed. In 1840 a further proposal emerged for a railway from Burntisland to Newport and Tayport, then called Ferryport on Craig, via Kinghorn, Kirkcaldy, Markinch and Cupar. The plans were not brought before Parliament until 1843 and were passed by both houses on 5 September 1845. The first sod of the Edinburgh and Northern Railway was cut at Kinghorn early the following year. Kirkcaldy Station opened on 20 June 1847 when the line was completed as far as Cupar, where a spur to Lindores formed part of an eventual link to Perth. Originally only the south platform was covered, and this Edwardian picture shows the station after improvements had been carried out in 1897.

The railway goods yard lies on an area shown on old maps as the Oven Acres. This 1912 picture was taken from the Bennochy Road bridge and shows the bustling yard in its heyday when it served the needs of the town's many manufacturing industries.

Kirkcaldy High School in St Brycedale Avenue was built in 1894 with money gifted by Michael B. Nairn. It replaced a building of 1843 in the town centre which had been built under the auspices of a trust bequeathed by Baillie Robert Philp, who died in 1828. This also provided for the setting up of schools in Linktown and Pathhead and partially funded Kinghorn burgh school. Restored after a serious fire in 1905, a technical wing was added to the building in 1926. The pupils moved to a new school at Dunnikier in 1958 and in 1964 the handsome building in this 1900 view was reduced to rubble. The technical wing was retained and is now part of Fife College of Technology, the nine-storey glass and concrete tower of which was built on the site of the high school in 1966.

St Brycedale U.F. Church, Kirkcaldy.

2113 J.V.

St Brycedale Church was completed between 1879 and 1881 to plans prepared by Aberdeen architect James Matthews. The identity of St Bryce, sometimes styled the patron saint of Kirkcaldy, remains a mystery, although one theory suggests that the name may be a form of St Bridget, also known as St Bride. Despite its continual omission from tourist brochures, the church contains two of the town's most important art treasures in the form of two stained glass windows designed by Edward Burne-Jones and executed by William Morris & Co. The first is entitled 'By the Waters of Babylon' and dates from 1889; the subject of the other one, completed three years later, is 'Moses and the Burning Bush and the Burial of Moses'.

An Episcopal congregation was formed in Kirkcaldy in 1811 and worshipped in a building in Coal Wynd. The foundation stone of St Peter's Church in Townsend Place, seen here in 1905, was laid in 1843. The building was found to have structural problems and its demolition and replacement were proposed in 1914, although in the event the decision was made to strengthen its foundations. A survey in 1976 found the church had been undermined by an old uncharted coal mine and it had to be pulled down.

In 1905 General William Booth, founder of the Salvation Army, embarked on a Scottish tour. He arrived in Kirkcaldy in the early hours of Monday 17 April and proceeded immediately to Beechwood (at the top of Bennochy Road), where he was entertained by Mrs Michael Beveridge. The photograph shows the general on the left and Mrs Beveridge in the centre. The sender has written that Booth had recently turned 77 and that 'Mrs B.' was exactly ten years older. After leaving Beechwood the general addressed a meeting of 3,000 people in the King's Theatre.

BALSUSNEY ROAD                                                          KIRKCALDY

The name Balsusney is said to derive from *baile-sassenach*, meaning the township of the Saxons. This study of Edwardian childhood is the work of Kirkcaldy photographer S. Heggie, who had a studio at 2 Thistle Street. His picture postcard views of the town have been found with postmarks spanning the years 1905 to 1908 and were produced by hand as contact prints, with the glass plate placed in direct contact with the photographic paper. This method produces pictures with extremely good definition and clarity. Examples of his work are very rare, and other Heggie postcards feature on the cover of this book and pages 12, 32, 39 and inside the back cover.

The annexation of most of the parish of Abbotshall in 1876 gave Kirkcaldy the opportunity to expand north of the railway, and Balsusney Road and its intersecting streets were built between this date and 1900. Octavia Street, little changed from this 1905 view, is named after Octavia Ellen Miles (1821-1907), wife of James Oswald of Dunnikier.

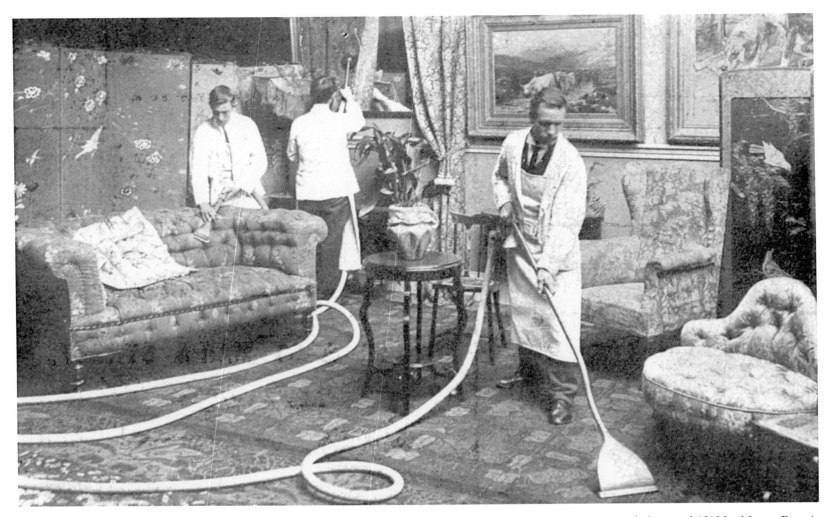

A housewife's dream – a small army of men in white coats to come and do the vacuuming. This service was provided around 1910 by Messrs Francis Duncan & Co. of 29-31 Maria Street, Kirkcaldy, as agents for the Scottish Vacuum Cleaner Co. Ltd. This illustration has been reproduced from an advertising postcard, and suggests that the three hoses were connected to a single vacuum unit.

Between 1876 and 1900 some 5,000 people settled in the new suburbs to the north of the town, creating an urgent need for additional school accommodation. The North Public School was designed by David Forbes Smith and opened in 1907, with places for 950 pupils. This contemporary postcard was published by John Davidson & Son of Kirkcaldy in their 'Ideal Series'.

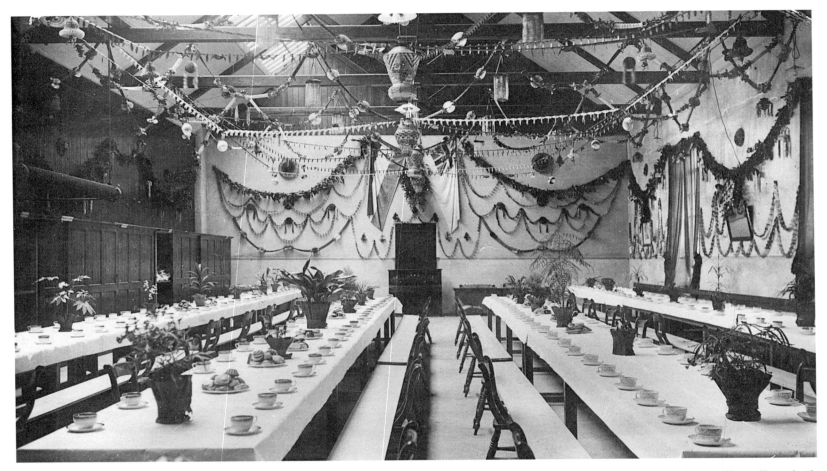

Another Davidson's postcard, showing Christmas decorations in the dining hall of the Caledonian Linen Mills in Montgomery Street. The mill was built in 1900 on an area of the Dunnikier Estate known as Spithead, for Robert Wemyss & Co. It was a replacement for their existing Abbotshall Mill, which stood until recently at the top of the Olympia Arcade. Robert Wemyss began making linen in 1837 in premises in Nicol Street and built the Abbotshall Mill in 1858, installing power looms two years later. The company manufactured linen and canvas for domestic and overseas markets and had important customers in New Zealand, Australia and South Africa. In 1956 the firm went into voluntary receivership and the factory was taken over by James Meikle, carpet manufacturer, who used it until they too went out of business in 1980 with the loss of 300 jobs.

A Church of Scotland congregation was formed in the Balsusney Road district in 1899 and was given permission to use the dining hall of the Caledonian Linen Mill for Sunday services. They were determined to build a church, but efforts in that direction were delayed by the Boer War. They subsequently acquired a site on the corner of Meldrum Road and Elgin Street, and the foundation stone of St John's Church was laid on 25 September 1907. The architect was William Williamson and the building was originally intended to have a square tower, but lack of funds prevented this from being built. St John's was completely destroyed by fire in the early hours of 19 September 1975.

A rare photograph showing the manufacture of aircraft wings in McIntosh's furniture factory in Victoria Road. The firm entered into a contract to make wings for De Havilland DH9 aircraft in February 1917 and work began on 2 April. The first sets were despatched on 1 September and by October the wings were being produced at a rate of seven to eight sets per week. Once the wooden frames were complete they were taken to Stocks' Mill in Linktown to be covered in canvas, before being returned to McIntosh's for finishing.

This photograph also shows De Havilland wings being made at McIntosh's in 1917. The firm was founded in 1869 by Alexander Henry McIntosh, in a small shop in Links Street. From there he moved to Rose Street and thence to Victoria Road, where he opened a large factory in 1880. By the 1920s the company was the largest manufacturer of furniture in Scotland. Their more notable contracts included making the furniture for the Cunard liners *Queen Mary* and *Queen Elizabeth I*. The firm moved to the Mitchelston Industrial Estate in 1970 and still trade today as E. S. A. McIntosh. Their former factory in Victoria Road was demolished to make way for the DHSS in 1976.

This photograph of the Kirkcaldy All Year Bathers, nicknamed the Polar Bears, was taken behind Anthony's Hotel in Linktown on 1 January 1905, shortly after they had completed their new year dip at Seafield. The group swam nude there every single day of the year before starting their work.

*Back row:*     D. Philp, J. Caysden, P. Quinn, Mr Dall, J. Ogilvie, Mr Tait.

*Third row:*     Mr Constable, J. Harcus, Wm. Yule, unknown, unknown, J. Kinnell, J. Michie, Mr Ferguson, Mr Watson, Mr Ingram.

*Second row:*     Mr Henderson, unknown, unknown, Mr Currie, Dr J. Sutherland Mackay (president of the club and burgh Medical Officer of Health), unknown, Mr Tait, unknown, J. Mill.

*Front:*     J. Philp, Mr Small.

In 1883 Parliament passed the Seafield Dock and Railway Act, granting a company of shareholders permission to erect a five acre dock enclosed by two piers at Seafield. The dock was primarily intended to gain a share of the growing export trade from the expanding Fife coalfields and was to be joined to the main line at Auchtertool by an eight mile railway. The project went no further at the time but was resurrected in 1888. Work began on the dock in February 1889. A large quantity of wood was brought from Kirkcaldy for shuttering the concrete piers and navvies arrived in the town anticipating work. However, after part of one pier was completed, the scheme was abandoned for good on 25 September 1889. The reason for this is not entirely clear, but may have been related to the opening in 1887 of the capacious Number 1 Dock at Methil, which lay closer to the most productive parts of the coalfield. This picture of the unfinished dock dates from 1905.

The Beach Seafield Kirkcaldy

Seafield beach, thronging with merrymakers in this mid-1900s view. The building flying the flag was the Seafield Cafe which advertised musical comedy and entertainers in summer. The Fife Coal Company attempted to mine here in 1924, but the results were disappointing and mining was abandoned after only three years. However, in 1954 the National Coal Board began preparatory work on a new deep mine to exploit reserves beneath the Forth. The twin winding towers were constructed in 1959 and production began in 1965. The Seafield Colliery closed in 1988 and the site was recently cleared and redeveloped with housing.